ECONOMY

EDITED BY NICK WINNICK

Weigl

CALGARY
www.weigl.com

Published by Weigl Educational Publishers Limited
6325 10 Street SE
Calgary, Alberta, Canada
T2H 2Z9

Website: www.weigl.com
Copyright ©2009 WEIGL EDUCATIONAL PUBLISHERS LIMITED

Library and Archives Canada Cataloguing in Publication data available upon request.
Fax (403) 233-7769 for the attention of the Publishing Records department.

ISBN 978-1-55388-492-7 (hard cover)
ISBN 978-1-55388-493-4 (soft cover)

Printed in the United States of America
1 2 3 4 5 6 7 8 9 0 12 11 10 09 08

All of the Internet URLs given in the book were valid at the time of publication. However, due to the dynamic nature of the Internet, some addresses may have changed, or sites may have ceased to exist since publication. While the author and publisher regret any inconvenience this may cause readers, no responsibility for any such changes can be accepted by either the author or the publisher.

Weigl acknowledges Getty Images as its primary image supplier for this title.

Every reasonable effort has been made to trace ownership and to obtain permission to reprint copyright material. The publishers would be pleased to have any errors or omissions brought to their attention so that they may be corrected in subsequent printings.

We acknowledge the financial support of the Government of Canada through the Book Publishing Industry Development Program (BPIDP) for our publishing activities.

EDITOR: Heather C. Hudak
DESIGN: Terry Paulhus

Through The Years

Since the beginning of the 20th century, the Canadian economy has faced major challenges and achieved great successes. From the spending sprees of the 1920s to the Great **Depression** of the 1930s, there have been extreme examples of "booms and busts" in the nation's financial history.

As the demand for certain products increase and supply diminishes, costs begin to skyrocket. Similarly, as products become more available, the price decreases making it more affordable for the general public. In an effort to stabilize the economy, governments try to predict these trends.

The political climate of the entire world has an impact on the Canadian economy—what happens in other parts of the world can directly affect prices and events at home. The World Wars overseas created a need for industry in Canada and required huge sums of money to fund. Importing and exporting products to and from other nations also contributes to the economic outlook of Canada.

Moving into the 21st century, Canada experienced some immediate economic challenges. As has always happened in the past, over time, the economy will shift, and these challenges will become opportunities.

2000s

Auto Woes

The early years of the 21st century saw the industry that had defined the 20th century beginning to struggle. High fuel prices and strong international competitors created problems for the North American auto industry. Many North Americans began buying smaller cars, and sales of trucks and sport utility vehicles fell. The Ontario economy was hit hard by this. The cities of Oakville and Oshawa held major truck manufacturing plants. In 2002, Ford announced plans to close its truck plant in Oakville, were unhappy about this turn of events. GM workers in particular noted that the move to close the truck plant violated their union contract. Canadian government and industry leaders continued to debate how best to aid the troubled auto industry.

Auto Woes

Oil on the Rise

2000s

Oil on the Rise

Many activities in Canada depend on inexpensive sources of energy. With Canadians spread out across a very large country, a great deal of time and energy is devoted to transportation of both people and goods. For the most part, these activities are powered by oil. In the late 2000s, the price of oil began to rise very quickly. From about $20 per barrel in 2000, it rose to $40 per barrel in 2004. Many political and economic factors contributed to this rise in price. Political instability in the Middle East, one of the world's largest oil producing regions, pushed the price still higher. In 2008, the record for the highest price of oil ever recorded was broken many times. In July of 2008, the price of oil exceeded $145 per barrel, more than seven times what it was at the beginning of the decade. Many Canadians began looking for ways to reduce their oil consumption. People began to purchase smaller vehicles that used less fuel. They also drove less often and less rapidly. The rise in the price of oil also created many business opportunities. Many forms of energy, such as solar and wind power, had been more expensive than oil in the early 2000s. With the rise in the price of oil, many of these "alternative" energies had a competitive price. Leaders in alternative energy fields were poised to contribute a great deal to the growth of the Canadian economy.

2004

Saskatchewan raises its Provincial Sales Tax by 1%

2005

A Wal-Mart store in Quebec threatens to close, just as its workers are about to create the first union contract with that company.

2000s

Return to Resources

Two of the biggest forces of economic growth in the world during the 2000s were China and India. Large workforces and the success of their manufacturing industries allowed these countries to begin new construction projects at rapid rates. This increased demand for Canada's natural resources. Non-precious metals, such as zinc, iron, nickel, and copper increased in value, due to their necessity in construction. Likewise, Canadian lumber and oil from Alberta's tar sands became increasingly prized on the international market. People moving to Alberta to take part in western Canada's resource boom. It was the largest inter-provincial migration in the nation's history. The migration was not without benefit, making Alberta's unemployment rate the lowest in the country at 3.4 percent. Canada continued to provide fuel to the world's economic engine.

2006

Inco Limited is bought out by Brazilian

2007

Protesters picket a trade meeting between North

Turbulence for Airlines

2003

Turbulence for Airlines

In the 2000s, flying became problematic for both airlines and passengers. Canada's largest airline, Air Canada, filed for **bankruptcy** protection in 2003. This meant that the company was in danger of collapsing, but that it would continue operating, in an attempt to pay off its debts. After 18 months, Air Canada emerged from bankruptcy protection, under the new ownership of ACE Aviation Holdings. ACE cut costs drastically, keeping Air Canada flying. However, other airlines were not able to recover. In 2003, a new airline called Jetsgo was created in Montreal. Jetsgo advertised low prices for its flights, and for a while, it delivered. However, in 2005, the company went bankrupt, almost overnight. Hundreds of passengers were stranded across Canada, and 1200 employees lost their jobs. The high price of oil in 2008 had a large impact on airlines, since jets use so much fuel. Every airline began looking for ways to save on fuel. Strategies included buying more efficient aircraft, removing heavy objects from airplanes, and flying more slowly. Even the largely successful Canadian airline, WestJet, was forced to alter its operation due to high fuel prices. There continues to be much uncertainty about the future of the industry, as oil prices continue to rise.

Into the Future

Throughout history, the Canadian economy has faced many periods of extreme growth, as well as hard times. What can we learn from the past about economic trends? What factors have contributed to economic booms and recessions?

| 2008 | 2009 | 2010 |

Economy
1990s

A Wealthy Barber

Balancing Budgets

Governments across Canada worked through the 1990s to balance their budgets. This meant they wanted to spend no more money than they took in through taxes. Business people liked this trend because it made governments operate more like businesses. Balanced government budgets encourage business people to invest money and make their businesses grow. This helps the economy grow by employing more people. Not everyone saw the balanced budgets as a good thing. Budgets are balanced by either spending less money or making more money. In most cases, governments chose to spend

Balancing Budgets

A Wealthy Barber

Next to the Bible, David Chilton's *The Wealthy Barber* is the best-selling book in Canadian history. The book tells the story of a barber and how he saves money. It teaches Canadians how to prepare for retirement. The book's main idea is to save just a small amount of money every month. The money should be invested in a Registered Retirement Savings Plan (RRSP). RRSPs pay interest regularly, so the money grows. Over time, the barber argues, even ordinary Canadians can become wealthy.

less money. Some people argued that this was the wrong choice. Cutbacks meant unemployed people no longer received as much money to live from programs such as welfare and Employment Insurance. In other cases, people paid the same or more money for less service. Many people were angry about decreases in health care because of cutbacks. Critics of spending cuts argued that governments should balance their budgets by taxing wealthy people more, not by spending less.

Gold Fever

It was a modern-day gold rush. Except this time people did not grab a gold pan and head for the hills. They phoned their stockbrokers and asked to invest in Bre-X Minerals. Bre-X was a Calgary company that claimed to have found a huge gold field in Indonesia in 1993. The amount of gold they claimed they found would have made it the largest gold find in the world. Thousands of people rushed to invest in the company. Many people became rich just by selling their stocks to other people. In 1996, the fever for gold ended. The geologist who made the first gold claims died mysteriously when he fell from a helicopter. Then a company that was partnered with Bre-X announced that there was no gold at all. Bre-X went broke within days, leaving behind only mystery and scandal.

Gold Fever

1993
An Alberta cow is found to be infected with mad cow disease.

1994
The NAFTA agreement goes into effect.

1995
Labatt is sold to Belgium's InBev.

11

Days of Action

1997

Days of Action

Ontario unions flexed their muscles in the fall of 1997. The Ontario Federation of Labour represented 650,000 unionized workers across the province. They organized a series of protests called Days of Action. Over a two-year period, nine city-wide strikes were held across the province. The Days of Action protested the provincial government's welfare and job cuts. The cutbacks were part of a program called the Common Sense Revolution. The "revolution" promised to reduce income tax and cut government spending. One demonstration in London, Ontario, drew 20,000 people. Another in Hamilton attracted 25,000 people. The walkout by 126,000 Ontario teachers was the longest illegal strike since the end of World War II. The teachers had enormous support. Parents and students joined striking teachers on the picket lines. Although the teachers went back to work without getting their demands, unions said public support made the protest a success.

1996
Ontario cuts the provincial income tax of its citizens by 30%.

1997
The Hibernia oil rig extracts its first barrel of crude oil.

1998
Royal Bank of Canada and Bank of Montreal attempt to merge.

Minimum Wage

Minimum Wage

In 1998, Alberta changed a law that had allowed companies to pay students under eighteen years old less than the minimum wage. Before the change, employers could pay students $4.50 per hour rather than the adult minimum wage of $5.00 per hour. Alberta also raised its minimum wage to $5.90 by the end of 1999. Ontario and the Northwest Territories continued to have laws that allowed employers to pay students a lower minimum wage than adults.

Minimum Wage	
British Columbia	$7.15
Alberta	$5.90
Saskatchewan	$5.60
Manitoba	$5.40
Ontario	$6.85
($6.40 for students)	
Quebec	$6.80
New Brunswick	$5.50
Nova Scotia	$5.50
Prince Edward Island	$5.40
Newfoundland	$5.25
Northwest Territories	$6.50
($6.00 for students)	
Yukon	$6.86

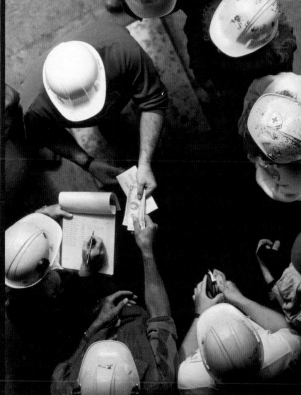

Into the Future

What is the minimum wage in your city or town? What was it when your parents or grandparents were young? Why do you think it has increased so much over time? How much do you think basic items like groceries or gasoline will cost in the future?

Canadian retail chain Eaton's files for bankruptcy.

Conrad Black's Hollinger sells most of its newspaper groups to CanWest.

Economy
1980s

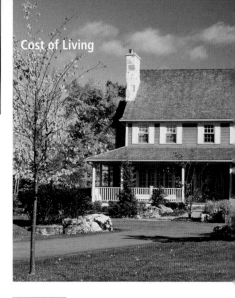

Cost of Living

1980s

Cost of Living

Cost of living means how much money is needed to provide people with homes, food, and other necessities. The cost of living increased greatly from the 1970s to the 1980s. House prices are one way to judge cost of living. From 1975 to 1985, the price of an average home nearly doubled across Canada.

Average Value of Canadian Homes

	1975	1985
Canada	$47,201	$80,775
Toronto	57,583	109,093
Vancouver	57,763	112,852
Mississauga	61,977	99,674
Victoria	n.a.	88,451
Hamilton	45,103	72,972
Ottawa	49,633	107,640
Calgary	48,341	80,462
Montreal	35,266	70,563
Edmonton	43,846	74,309
Halifax	n.a.	79,350
St. John's	n.a.	66,642
Winnipeg	33,463	62,478
Saint John	35,884	57,088
Regina	33,880	61,403

1980s

The National Energy Program

In 1975, most of the Canadian oil industry was owned by people other than Canadians. In 1980, the Canadian government announced a new program to help keep money made from oil and gas in Canada. The National Energy Program (NEP) was made up of three parts. First, the government included its own oil company, PetroCanada, which was created in 1976. It also became more difficult for foreign oil companies to start up in Canada. Second, the government made sure that Canadians could buy oil at prices well under what it was selling for around the world. Third, the government wanted the money made from oil and gas to go to the federal government, not to the provinces. From the moment the NEP was announced, western Canadians were against it.

1981
Canada Post becomes a government-owned organization.

1982
The first Lotto 6/49 draw is held— the winner receives $500,000.

1983
The North American Salmon Conservation Organization is created.

The National Energy Program

The oil-rich provinces of the West were forced to sell their oil at lower prices for **domestic** sales. Alberta in particular did not think that the government had a right to interfere in the oil industry. Much of the province's wealth came from oil and gas. The Alberta government accused the federal government of interfering with its powers.

Albertans felt robbed by the NEP. When Brian Mulroney was elected in 1984, he met with the premiers of the western provinces. Soon after, the NEP ended.

1980s

The GST

Although the Canadian government would not start collecting money from the new federal goods and services tax (GST) until 1991, the tax was announced in the summer of 1989. Most provinces already collected provincial taxes on goods and services. The new tax meant that goods and services in Canada would cost 7 percent more. The extra money would go to the federal government to help it run programs for Canadians.

The GST

Recession in Canada

1982

Recession in Canada

Canada did not fall into an economic depression in the eighties. Instead, it suffered from a recession. A recession is a period of lowered economic activity. During the 1980s, more Canadians had trouble finding jobs than ever before. The unemployment rate reached 12.9 percent in December 1982. This was higher than it had been since the Depression in the 1930s. The value of the Canadian dollar dropped compared to the U.S. dollar. In 1986, the Canadian dollar was worth 70.2 U.S. cents, which was less internationally than it ever had in history. This was just the beginning of a trend that would see the dollar drop much lower during the next decade.

1984

Canadian TV channels MuchMusic and TSN hit the airwaves, competing with U.S. sports and music broadcasting.

1985

Potentially tainted tuna makes its way to store shelves in Canada.

1982

Devine Government

In 1982, Grant Devine and the Progressive Conservative party were elected to run the Saskatchewan government. Premier Devine stayed in power until 1991. This **Tory** government is now considered one of the most corrupt in Canadian history. While in power, Premier Devine created a huge **deficit** for Saskatchewan. As it was later discovered, many of the cabinet members were guilty of lying or stealing money from the government. In all, twenty-one members of the Saskatchewan government were charged with crimes committed during the 1980s. Premier Grant Devine was not directly linked to any of the crimes. However, the government was not all greed and corruption. In an effort to keep the people of Saskatchewan at work during a nation-wide recession, the government developed the Home-owners Grant. It offered money to people to fix up their homes, yards, and neighbourhoods. The government's hope for this project was to foster pride of ownership, neighbourhood development, and the employment of people in a variety of fields. Hospitals were also built across the province for many of the same reasons.

1987

The Loonie

In 1987, the Canadian government produced the eleven-sided one-dollar coin. The coin was nicknamed the "loonie" because of the loon on one of its sides. At first, some Canadians did not like the idea of carrying a heavy coin instead of a dollar bill. Other Canadians were excited by the idea of a new coin. Soon after the coin appeared, the one-dollar bills disappeared and loonies became commonplace.

The Loonie

1986

The Canadian dollar dips to 70 percent of the value of the U.S. dollar.

1987

Canadian and U.S. Free Trade Agreement negotiations are finalized.

Black Monday

1987

Black Monday

On October 19, 1987, the New York Stock Exchange had its lowest drop in history. This meant that many people lost a great deal of money in one day. The loss was even worse than the Wall Street crash of 1929 that was the start of the Great Depression. Luckily, the world economy did not suffer from another depression.

Into the Future

During times of economic decline, businesses often find it hard to remain profitable. Think about the businesses in your community. When did they first open? Have any closed? What makes a business successful? Are there any businesses that would do especially well in your neighborhood?

1988

Facilities for the 1988 Olympics in Calgary cost $400 million to build.

1989

The Canadian government makes major cuts to VIA Rail.

1990

The National Gallery buys *Voice of Fire* for $1.8 million.

Foreign Investment in Canada in Millions of Dollars

France	475
Germany	364
Japan	103
Netherlands	452
Sweden	126
Switzerland	353
United Kingdom	2,641
United States	22,054
Total	26,568

1970s

Foreign Investment

Other countries also affected Canada's economy. In the 1970s, this became a concern.

1970s

Controls out of Control

During wartime, wages and prices were often controlled. Canada's only experience with such regulations in peacetime, however, occurred between 1975 and 1978. There were high **inflation** rates in 1974. Inflation measures the increase in the price level. In response to the levels, the Anti-Inflation Act set a three-year controls system. Wages were set, and prices and markups for products were restricted. Wages had to stay the same, and this restriction applied to all companies with more than 500 employees, all government agencies, and most public service offices. Prime Minister Trudeau promised during the election that he would not enact these controls. He went back on his word in 1975 by setting the restrictions. While Canadians disagreed with these measures, the controls did reduce inflation in a way that was otherwise not possible.

Foreign Investment

1971
Canada's first CANDU nuclear reactor goes online

1972
Donald Macdonald becomes the first non-European to lead the International **Confederation** of Free-Trade Unions

Controls out of Control

The Power of Water

The James Bay Project was planned to be an incredible hydroelectric-power development. However, it ran into problems from the start. The initial project cost $15 million, and it diverted water from several rivers into a reservoir. Since its announcement in 1971, the Cree First Nations fought against it because of the impact on the environment and their land. There was a great deal of money at stake, so the government tried to come to an agreement with the Cree.

The Power of Water

Four years later, the Cree gave up their land claims for $225 million, and they were given special hunting and fishing rights. The phases of the James Bay Project continued through the seventies and eighties.

1973
OPEC's raises benefitting Alberta's economy.

1974
French becomes the official language of all business conducted in Quebec.

1975
Canada prevents Soviet fishing boats from entering Canadian waters.

The New Canadian Work Force

coastal border out to 200 nautical miles (about 320 kms) from the shore. The fishing zone and a ban on commercial salmon fishing were conservation measures that were disastrous to Atlantic Canadians. Many of the area's fishers had been fishing for fifty years, and they had no other means to make a living. New Brunswick had experienced layoffs and business closures, causing record unemployment six months prior to the fishing ban. The regulations caused both an economic and psychological blow to Atlantic fishers.

"All the fishermen have is their small homes, a small bit of land for a garden plot and their boats and fishing gear. Even if the government buys up their gear as they have said they will do, it won't solve the problems of these men." Harper Smith, president of New Bandon Fishermen's Association.

1971

The New Canadian Work Force

The people contributing to the Canadian economy continued to change in the seventies. With the rise of feminism in the sixties and seventies, more women joined the work force. Since 1946, female participation in the economy rose from 24.7 percent to 51.6 percent. Despite this increase, in 1971 women earned only 58 percent of what men earned doing the same job. Women organized, joined unions, and demanded equal pay and working conditions. They also wanted their economic, social, and political positions in society to be recognized.

1972

Fish Stocks in Trouble

In 1972, Fisheries Minister Jack Davis tried to push Canada's

Fish Stocks in Trouble

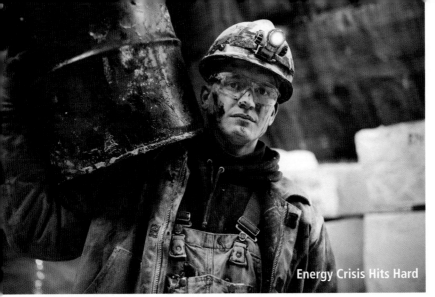

Energy Crisis Hits Hard

Energy Crisis Hits Hard

From October 1973 to March 1974, there was an oil **embargo** by the Arab members of the Organization of Petroleum Exporting Countries (OPEC). They were protesting the United States' military support of Israel in the 1973 Middle East war. This caused economic concern and uncertainty across the country. There were concerns over whether Canada had enough oil and gas resources for the future. The world oil prices increased 160 percent in 1979,

and Canada raised its prices to compete with the world oil prices. This did not make the United States happy because the U.S. bought oil from Canada. The energy crisis also caused eight years of conflict in Canada. The crisis created a debate over what the price of oil within Canada should be and who received the profits from the sale of oil outside Canada's borders.

Alberta, the major producer of oil and gas in Canada, claimed that the rights to oil and gas were provincial, and they wanted to be able to sell gas at a competitive price. This would mean a jump in prices for

Canadian consumers. The federal government argued that the Canadian constitution suggested a partnership, and the entire country should share in the good fortune. Alberta Premier, Peter Lougheed disagreed and promised to fight against any attempt to force such controls. The debate raged on. It was not until 1980 that the provincial and federal dispute was settled. The federal government allowed for a gradual price increase in oil prices over five years. John Poyen, president of The Canadian Petroleum Association, said, "We are seriously concerned that the oil industry which takes all the risks is now being denied the opportunity to obtain full market values for its production."

Into the Future

In the 1970s, the price of oil skyrocketed, causing many people to look for less expensive modes of transportation and more efficient ways to heat their homes. Look at energy costs today. Are they more affordable than in the 1970s? Do people still look for more affordable ways to acquire energy? Why?

1978
Inco workers in Sudbury, Ontario, begin a strike that would last nine months

1979
Canada begins the sale of a gold bullion coin

1980
Canadian Steamship Lines Inc. is sold to future Prime Minister Paul Martin

Economy
1960s

Newfoundland Outport Residents Resettled

Fishers and their families were encouraged to move from tiny coastal villages to "growth centres," where it was hoped manufacturing and industry would develop. Large fish-processing plants put many of the independent fisheries out of business. Moreover, the government no longer wanted to provide education, health, and other services to the isolated outposts. Many of the residents were reluctant to leave their traditional way of life.

Canadian Magazines

Canadian magazines have always faced heavy competition from American magazines. In 1961, the Royal Commission of Publications reported that three-quarters of the general-interest magazines sold in Canada were American

Canadian Magazines

Newfoundland Outport Residents Resettled

1961	1962	1963
The National Oil Policy	The Globe and Mail begins	The Trans-Canada

publications. It also found that Time and *Reader's Digest*, two popular American magazines, took 40 cents of every dollar spent on magazine advertising. The commission recommended that foreign magazines should not be allowed to carry Canadian advertisements aimed at the Canadian market. It also suggested that Canadian companies advertising in foreign magazines should not get the same tax breaks as those advertising in Canadian magazines. Prime Minister Diefenbaker accepted these recommendations, though he excluded *Time* and *Reader's Digest* from the new arrangement. By 1970, *Reader's Digest's* circulation had climbed from 1 million to 1.5 million, and *Time's* from 215,000 to 444,000. In the same period, *Time's* advertising **revenue** tripled.

Hydro-Québec

1962

Potash Mining in Saskatchewan

Potash is an essential ingredient in fertilizers. In 1962, drilling began at Esterhazy, Saskatchewan, the world's largest potash mine. Two years later, another mine opened near Regina. Potash exports quickly became important in the provincial economy.

1962

Hydro-Québec

When the Quebec government nationalized 11 private electric power companies in 1962, they were absorbed by Hydro-Québec. This company was owned by the province of Quebec and was Canada's largest electric utility company. It provides Quebec with power, and exports surplus power to the United States. In 1969, Hydro-Québec contracted to buy power from the Churchill Falls project in Labrador until the year 2041 at the price fixed in 1969.

Potash Mining in Saskatchewan

Canadian Wealth

Alberta Oil Sands

Fort McMurray is the centre of the Alberta oil sands, an area with an estimated 3.9 billion cubic metres of synthetic crude oil. In 1964, the Great Canadian Oil Sands project was given the go-ahead. Fort McMurray immediately became a boom town. By the end of the decade, its population had quadrupled. Sun Oil invested $300 million in a plant to produce oil piped to Edmonton.

1964

Canadian Wealth

Canada was considered the second most affluent country in the world after the United States, according to the Organization for Economic Cooperation and Development. The 1964 survey found that one in four Canadians owned radio sets and one in 3.47 owned cars.

1965

Canada Pension Plan

It took twenty-six days of debate, but Canada finally had a national pension plan. The House of Commons approved the Canada

Alberta Oil Sands

WELCOME TO FORT McMURRAY
WE HAVE THE ENERGY

1966
The Montreal Metro opens for business

1967
The government emphasizes training programs for workers to combat unemployment

1968
The laws that would become the Medicare system are written

24

Canada Pension Plan

Postal Strike

On July 22, 1965, 20,000 unionized postal workers went on strike. They stayed off the job for eighteen days. It was one of the largest "wildcat" strikes in Canadian history, and the largest involving government employees. The workers did not win all their wage demands, but Prime Minister Pearson agreed that **collective bargaining** would be allowed in the future in public service. That meant that government employees

Postal Strike

would have the right to go on strike on issues such as higher wages, job security, job classification, and the use of casual and part-time workers.

Pension Plan on March 29, 1965. Employees would contribute 1.8 percent of their income to the plan, to a maximum of $5,000 annually. Employers would match that amount. During the sixties, pension benefits could reach $104 a month, starting at the age of seventy.

Into the Future

Having a healthy economy involves more than just earning high wages. Funding from governments and donors for services, such libraries, hospitals, and schools, contributes to a healthy economy. Think about your community. What services are funded through donors or the government? Would you be willing to pay for these services if funding was no longer available? What other services would you like to have in your community?

Economy
1950s

Booming Economy

Booming Economy

The 1950s were great times for Canada. There were plenty of jobs, and people had money to spend. In Ontario and Quebec especially, new factories and businesses employed thousands of people. Many others found work in the forestry and mining industries. Even parts of the country that had been hit hard by the Depression of the 1930s were doing well. In Atlantic Canada, for instance, numerous businesses were started. As well, the new, large military base at Gagetown, New Brunswick, provided many jobs. However, the picture was not so bright in Newfoundland, where most people still had a hard time making a living. By contrast, western Canada was booming. Alberta was doing especially well because of the huge deposits of oil and gas that had been discovered there. Copper and zinc, and **uranium** mines were adding to Saskatchewan's revenue, while new hydroelectric plants and other developments were bringing jobs to British Columbia and Manitoba. The outlook was also good for prairie farmers, because the federal government was selling large quantities of wheat abroad.

Equal Pay for Some Women

1950s

Equal Pay for Some Women

As a rule, men earned far more than women. In 1950, for example, the average salary of a Canadian man was $2,419. For a Canadian woman, it was $1,376. Many people thought this was fair and proper. "Men have to support a family," they said. "Men ought to get paid more." Women's groups disagreed, and they pressed for change. They had some success in 1951, when the Ontario government passed a law stating that women must be paid the same as men if they did the same job. Five years later, the federal government passed a similar law, but it applied only to people working for the federal government.

1953

The Trans Mountain Oil Pipeline is completed

1954

The first Alberta oil arrives in Sarnia via a new pipeline

1955

Toronto-Dominion Bank is formed by the merger of The Bank of Toronto and Dominion Bank

1954

Huge Uranium Find at Elliot Lake

In 1954, the discovery of uranium at Elliot Lake, Ontario, sparked a mining boom. People flocked to the area. At a height of the boom, mine-shaft drillers could earn as much as $1,200 a month—around six times the average Canadian salary. Before long, there were eleven mines in operation, including Consolidated Denison, the world's largest uranium mine.

1959

Avro Arrow Cancelled

"It can't be true!" said an aircraft mechanic. But it was true. In February 1959, Prime Minister Diefenbaker cancelled all work on Canada's famous jet fighter plane, the Avro Arrow. He said it was costing too much. The military no longer seemed interested in fighter planes as missiles seemed to be a better defence. The whole project was scrapped. The few planes already built were to be destroyed, said Diefenbaker. This was a major blow to Canada's aircraft industry. The Arrow was a magnificent plane. Test flights had indicated it would be one of the fastest fighter planes in the world, reaching almost twice the speed of sound. There had been talk of building 600 Arrows, and now not even one would exist. Around 14,000 people lost their jobs.

Huge Uranium Find at Elliot Lake

1956

The Canadian Labour Congress is formed

1957

The Canada Council for the Arts is formed

1958

The underwater hazard "Ripple Rock" is destroyed, making seagoing trade much safer in the Vancouver area

Avro Arrow Cancelled

Into the Future

Events that take place around the world often have a direct affect on the Canadian economy. If there is a war in oil-rich countries, your parents may pay more to fill their car with fuel. Poor weather in China may harm rice crops, raising the price you pay for this staple food. Think about events taking place around the world today. Do they affect the economy where you live? How?

| 1959 | 1960

Economy
1940s

Canada Booms While Allies Bust

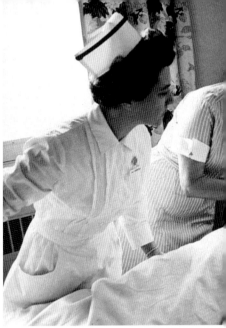

new families, which created great demand in many industries, but the boom had a cost, too. The demand for goods and a population increase because of immigration caused an increase in imports of U.S. goods. The number of Canadian exports to Europe before the war, decreased. Canada grew more dependent on the United States to meet its citizens' demands. By 1950, the economies in Europe had recovered, and these problems disappeared. Canada's economic boom continued.

1940s

Canada Booms While Allies Bust

Industry in Canada took off during the war. European and Asian countries were not strong economically. This opened more markets to which Canadian manufacturers could sell. After the war, industry was switched to peacetime products. New homes were built as quickly as post-war material shortages would allow. There were many

1940s

Social Welfare Introduced

No one wanted Canada to experience the suffering it had during the 1930s' Great Depression. To prevent this from happening, the government created a safety net for the poor.

1941

Metalworkers at the Alcan facility in Arvida, Quebec, go on strike.

1942

Canada produces more than 4,000 aircraft annually.

Social Welfare Introduced

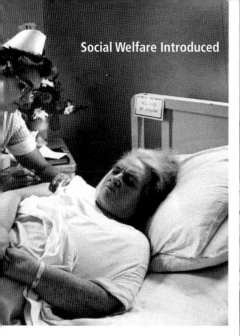

Wartime Prices and Trade Board Sets Controls

In 1943, The Unemployment Insurance Act called for social security through family allowance and health coverage. Also, Saskatchewan's hospital plan of 1945 covered every provincial resident. Its success caused other provinces to follow its lead. In the same year, the government offered the provinces a grant for the development of medical and hospital insurance. The government also suggested old-age pensions for Canadians over the age of seventy, and a cost-shared pension for people between sixty-five and sixty-nine years old. The government was to take responsibility for the unemployed. Arguments between the provincial and federal governments over how to share the cost could not be solved. The plans were put on hold. In 1951, universal old-age pensions were brought into effect.

1940s

Wartime Prices and Trade Board Sets Controls

The Wartime Prices and Trade Board was established in 1939. It took control of prices and wages. The government wanted to prevent the rising costs that occurred during World War I. The organization created plans to distribute goods that were not easily found. The shortages that occurred during the 1940s were frustrating for workers. They were finally making money after surviving the Great Depression, but there was little they could buy. Even into peacetime, Canadians supported the wartime wage and price controls. It showed the confidence Canadians had in the government and the fairness of the controls system. Canadians also supported the war effort through bonds. Canada Savings Bonds came out of the success of Victory Bonds and were sold throughout the rest of the century.

1943
Unemployment rates fall as the wartime economy booms.

1944
Canadian exports reach $1.2 billion in value.

1945
The budget deficit rises to 43 percent, but unemployment is less than 1 percent. **31**

Canadians Look After Families

on Tariffs and Trade (GATT). The organization aimed to free up how countries traded with each other. Each country had to give other member countries the same deals on tariffs as it gave to its best trading partner. Canada negotiated with seven of the member countries. The talks between Canada and the United States were the most intensive. The 1930s agreements between the two neighbours were replaced by GATT conditions. The rules were clear, but there were exceptions. Preferences that existed before GATT could be kept in place. Canada kept the trade benefits it received from the Britain Commonwealth preferences. But some exceptions were against Canada's interests. Agricultural products were not included in the trade agreement. Canada and other agricultural exporters objected.

1945

Canadians Look After Families

In 1945, the government began a family allowance program, which included a "baby bonus" to every family. This allotted money for each child to make sure he or she was cared for. The money was intended to help families pay for medical and dental expenses, food, and housing for children under sixteen years old. This applied to all families in the country, including wealthy families that did not need the help. Families that made more money were taxed on the family allowance assistance. They also received only a percentage of the possible amount. The government gave lower-income families $5 a month for each child under six and $8 for a child between thirteen and fifteen. The program cost $250 million to operate during the first year alone.

1947

GATT Established

In 1947, twenty-two countries signed the General Agreement

GATT Established

1946
Canada Savings Bonds make their debut.

1947
A new oil discovery is made in Leduc, Alberta.

1948
Louis Saint Laurent is elected prime minister.

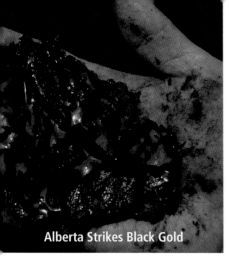

Alberta Strikes Black Gold

Asbestos Strike

1947

Alberta Strikes Black Gold

In 1947, oil was discovered in Leduc, Alberta. The Leduc field was larger than the nearly spent one in Turner Valley. In the following years, even bigger oil fields were discovered. Exploration in Alberta, Saskatchewan, and Manitoba unearthed new oil and gas reserves. The oil boom led to growth in other industries as well. Drilling required that plants and pipelines be built. Canada was now able to support its own energy needs.

February 1949

Asbestos Strike

In February 1949, Quebec asbestos workers walked off the job. The four-month strike brought major asbestos mines to a halt. Asbestos mining was an important industry and the walk-out cost companies a lot of money. Five thousand workers were part of the illegal strike. Previously, the union had cooperated with management. The workers and the Confederation of National Trade Unions now challenged the way unions were run and the English management of Quebec mines. The strike, which had a few violent clashes with police, finally ended in July, but it was the start of an era of labour conflict in Quebec.

Into the Future

World War II had a huge impact on economies around the world, including Canada's. How did the country pay for its war efforts? How did it help to rebuild afterward? Today, wars continue to take place around the world. How does Canada aid its international neighbours in times of both war and peace?

1949

Canada's largest Great Lakes passenger ship is destroyed in a fire.

1950

A strike among Canada's rail workers brings the economy to a virtual standstill.

Economy
1930s

Rotten Potatoes, Rotten Tomatoes

During the Great Depression, Canadians had too much of everything except money and jobs. In Prince Edward Island, potatoes were left to rot in the soil because no one could afford to buy them. The same was true of tomatoes in British Columbia. The problem was that because of their financial problems, farmers could not buy such items as farm equipment, seeds, fertilizer, and clothes. The stores that usually sold these goods were left with full shelves. Stores stopped ordering goods from manufacturers. With fewer orders, manufacturers laid off workers. These workers could no longer afford to buy things. This led to more lay-offs. People stopped believing that things would get better. People drove older cars and stopped going to doctors and dentists to save money. They wore patched clothes. Children went barefoot in the summer and saved their socks to use as gloves in the winter. Flour sacks made good underwear, and cardboard filled holes in shoes. People saved money any way they could.

Rotten Potatoes, Rotten Tomatoes

1931
Beauharnois Power gives the Liberal party $700,000 for the rights to dam a river.

1932
The crown corporation that would eventually become the CBC is created.

The Great Depression

The Great Depression was one of the worst economic times in history. It affected countries around the world. Countries that normally bought Canadian wheat, fish, wood, and automobiles could no longer afford to do so. Eighty percent of Canada's farm, forest, and mine products were sold abroad, so Canada was hurt when countries stopped buying its products.

Funky Income

Before the depression, a Maritime company had tried to raise skunks for their pelts. When the public showed no interest in skunk fur, the forty animals were set free. Soon, Prince Edward Island was overrun with skunks. The government offered 50 cents per skunk snout. This was one way to earn money during the Depression. Some people even went to Nova Scotia to illegally trap skunks. One imaginative person made fake snouts from cow hide. In three years, the government paid bounties on over 15,000 skunks.

The Great Depression

Funky Income

1933
Newfoundland gives up control to Great Britain.

1934
The president of the Labatt Brewing Company is kidnapped and released three days later.

1935
Poor economic conditions spark a youth riot in Regina.

Working Conditions

Since so many people were unemployed, companies were able to force their employees to work long hours for low wages. When factories were busy, employees worked over 60 hours a week, including Saturday. There was no overtime pay. As one worker noted, "you were like firemen—you were always on call." Jobs were difficult to obtain. When an Edmonton store advertised for salesgirls, the next day hundreds of women formed a line that circled the entire block. Since the store only had three positions available, there was a riot. Some companies made a fortune. They paid their employees very little and charged high prices for their goods. A government commission found, for example, that while Eaton's paid seamstresses 9.5 cents for sewing a dozen dresses, each dress was sold for $1.59.

The Hard Numbers

Average Yearly Income Per Person

	1928	1933
British Columbia	$590	$310
Alberta	$550	$210
Saskatchewan	$480	$140
Manitoba	$470	$240
Ontario	$550	$310
New Brunswick	$290	$180
Nova Scotia	$320	$210
PEI	$280	$150
Canada	**$470**	**$250**

Working Conditions

1936	1937	1938
Rodeo entrepreneur Earl Bascom begins building rodeo grandstands in the United States.	Trans-Canada Airlines is created.	Joe Shuster and Jerry Siegal create the **Superman** character.

On Strike

1936

On Strike

In 1936, workers at the Kelsey Wheel Company in Windsor, Ontario, decided they had had enough. They took part in Canada's first sit-down strike against low wages, long hours, and dangerous working conditions. This meant workers sat at their machines and would not work or leave. While not a total success, they won some of their demands. Such tactics were not always successful. A Sarnia, Ontario, company sent in men to beat strikers with baseball bats. Police and the government took the company's side and would not protect the strikers. In 1937, there were 278 strikes in 125 communities. One of the most significant strikes took place at General Motors in Oshawa, Ontario. Although General Motors had increased its profits the previous year, it cut wages for the fifth time in five years. Workers walked off the job in protest. They demanded the right to join a union and have the union negotiate better wages on their behalf. They also wanted a rest period, a regular work week, and time and a half wages for overtime work. The company refused these demands at first. However, it began to fear that other companies would take much of its business if the strike lasted too long. After 15 days, the company gave in and the workers returned to their jobs.

Into the Future

During the Great Depression, many items that people use daily were difficult to acquire. Food and clothing were rationed, and jobs were hard to find. What would it be like to live during this time? How is this different from today?

1939

Canadian troops in Europe are joined by radio broadcasters, who set up the Radio Canada International service.

1940

Unemployment Insurance is first introduced.

Changing Times in Canada

Inflation Hits Canada Hard

Changing Times in Canada

Many people were unemployed in the early 1920s. The country battled a recession and lost. By 1924, the economy began to improve. Canada was rich in natural resources, and this helped turn around the economy. Forest products, gold, silver, zinc, lead, copper, and water power became necessary for the Canadian economy. Canada had such a large supply of nickel that in 1922 the government changed the five-cent piece from silver to nickel.

Canadian Exports

The great majority of Canada's exports were products of our natural resources. In 1929, for example, our leading exports were:

Product	% of Total Exports
Wheat	32
Paper	11
Flour	5
Lumber boards	4
Automobiles	3
Fish	3
Copper	2
Barley	2
TOTAL	62

1921
The United Farmers of Alberta party wins a majority of seats in that province's legislature

1922
France gives Canada the land around Vimy Ridge.

1923
Canada signs the Halibut Treaty with the United States

1920s

Inflation Hits Canada Hard

The first half of the decade was a period of economic depression. Many people were unemployed. Soldiers who returned from fighting for Canada in World War I were unable to find work. Inflation quickly ate through people's life savings as prices rose higher and higher.

1920s

Working Women

Help around the house until you get married. If you have to work, hand over your paycheque to your parents. These were the rules about women and work in the 1920s. At the beginning of the decade, around 17 percent of all women over the age of fifteen earned a wage. Very few women were allowed to be doctors, dentists, lawyers, school principals, engineers, or company executives. Most were store clerks, secretaries, domestic servants, or factory workers. One woman recalled her experience with her father when she wanted to work. "When I got out of high school, the first thing I wanted to be was a nurse, so I went to the family doctor and he told me, 'Go home.' He was the same as my father,

you see. So I went to business college....I got a job [in a hotel], and my father phoned them and said I was too young and got me fired....Then I got a job peeling potatoes in the YMCA

up at Banff. He wouldn't let me do that either. He wouldn't let me do any of those things. You were just supposed to be around the house until you got married. He wasn't even going to let me drive the car."

A Single Woman's Weekly Budget in 1929	
Food	$ 8.00
Room	2.50
Washing	1.00
Car fare	.75
Insurance	.50
Clothes, toiletries	3.75
Reading, letters	1.00
Loss of time for sickness, holidays	1.00
Medicine, dentist, doctor	.50
Saving for old age, unemployment	1.00

1924

Several members of the Ontario government are found guilty of embezzlement in the Ontario Bond Scandal.

1925

Canada and the United States sign the Lake of the Woods treaty.

1920

Newsprint Boom

America's reading habits provided a needed boost to the Canadian economy. The growth of education in the late 19th century created a new, large group of readers. Newspaper reading increased greatly. By the end of the decade, Americans were buying 93 million newspapers. Soon, the average paper doubled in thickness due mostly to increased advertisements in the papers. The Sunday paper began during the decade. It included illustrations, supplements, and book reviews. Each issue was up to 160 pages thick. The weekend edition of the Chicago Tribune required 50,000 tonnes of newsprint each year. Since large American cities were easily accessible to Canada by rail or waterway, Americans looked north for most of their newsprint. By mid-decade, Canada was the world's largest supplier of newsprint. In 1920, Canada produced over 900 tonnes of newsprint. By the end of the decade, it reached almost 3,000 tonnes. Although Nova Scotia, New Brunswick, and Manitoba each had plenty of sawmills, the largest pulp and paper producers were based in other provinces. Quebec produced half, Ontario produced around one-third, and British Columbia produced one-tenth of the paper.

1926
Canada returns its currency to the gold standard.

1927
The Canada Pension Plan is created.

1928
An economic booms lasts well into 1928.

Labour Unrest

"War is on," declared the Nova Scotia coal miners' union in June 1923. Not all parts of the country had grown at the same pace, and the Maritimes lagged behind the rest of the country. Here, the coal industry fell on hard times and a series of long, violent strikes left the region unhappy. In 1922, the miners' wages had been reduced by one-third. In the summer of 1923, more than 22,000 miners went on strike in Cape Breton. They wanted higher wages, an eight-hour day, and recognition of their union. To break the strike, the government sent in the military to support the company. Several times, the troops fired over the heads of angry strikers.

Labour Unrest

The company cancelled all credit at its stores, which were often the only stores in the area. Strikers had to give in.

Even though the city councils supported the miners, the mining companies came out on top.

Into the Future

Canada's workforce today looks very different from the way it did in the 1920s. Many more women and new Canadians hold positions in the workplace now. What do you think makes these changes so slow to happen? Are there any ideas today that might prevent people from achieving equality in their working lives?

1929
The New York Stock Exchange crashes, beginning the Great Depression.

1930
Canada and the United States raise tariffs.

41

War Boom

Canadian Slums

1910s

Inflation Brings Higher Wages

The rate of inflation skyrocketed in the mid-to late-1910s. It was twice that of wages between 1916 and 1919. Prices increased by 8 percent in 1916, 18 percent in 1917, and 13.5 percent in 1918. Workers could not keep up with the cost of living. Western Canada was hit hard by inflation. Alberta miners fought for higher wages in August 1916. The Western Coal Operators' Association and the United Mine Workers of America signed an agreement with workers for more money. Mine operators also agreed not to hire cheap.

1910s

War Boom

The start of World War I added a needed boost to Canada's economy. The high

Inflation Brings Higher Wages

unemployment came down. The value of products needed to make war goods rose quickly. Metals, wood, and newsprint were in demand. Canada also exported meat and wheat. Meat exports went from $6 million to $85 million, and trade in livestock rose from $10 million to $25 million. Canadian manufacturing produced much of Great Britain's ammunition, weaponry, and other war supplies. This gave Canada a $1 billion boost, and it put more than 300,000 more people to work during the war years. But in the end, the borrowing done to finance the war came back to haunt Canadians. The debt rose from $463 million to $2.46 billion.

1912

Paper Business Booms in British Columbia

After three years of construction, the Powell River Company was finally ready to start business. In April 1912, the company on the British Columbia coast produced its first roll of

1910s

Canadian Slums

During the 1910s, large Canadian centres were home to thousands of people, many of whom were very poor. It was not uncommon to have thirty people living in a boarding house with four rooms. People did not have anywhere else to sleep or live. They could not afford a house of their own, so they had to find a roof over their heads in any way they could. Families often shared one bed, and many children were left to fend for themselves. Some children collected coal from beside railway cars so their families had something to burn to stay warm.

1912

The first and last Amherst automobiles are manufactured in Calgary.

1914

Western Canada's first major oil discovery occurs in Turner Valley, Alberta.

Paper Business Booms in British Columbia

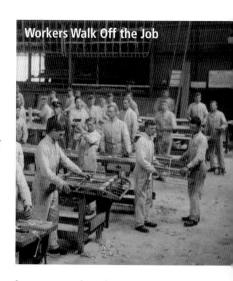
Workers Walk Off the Job

The oil was found 810-metres under the ground, and A.W. Dingman, a Toronto engineer, said it was high-grade oil. He cautioned people that the initial gusher did not necessarily mean it would continue to gush for a long time. His words fell on deaf ears. People rushed to oil brokers in hopes of buying oil shares. The value of oil stocks hit the ceiling when news of the gusher was released. Seven drilling companies were at work in the area, which was know to be rich in oil. The Dingman discovery started the oil boom in Alberta. The industry remained relatively small until a major oil find in Leduc in 1947.

newsprint. Newspapers including Vancouver's Province printed some issues on the new business' paper. The company was owned by American businessmen who were leaders in the development of this natural resource. The sawmill was built, as was a town for the workers. The paper industry was a boost to the economy, but some people were fearful. They felt that the American companies did not care about British Columbia and that they were exploiting the timber resources in the region.

1913

Oil Fever

The Calgary-area Dingman well struck oil in 1913. Everyone was excited by what the find meant. But that frenzy was nothing compared to the one in 1914. The well drilled into a pocket, sending oil gushing into the air.

1919

Workers Walk Off the Job

What began as a disagreement over wages and collective bargaining in the building and metal trades soon became a huge strike that affected all of western Canada. Metal workers, carpenters, and brick

Oil Fever

layers turned to the Winnipeg Trades and Labour Council for help. The council called for a vote on a sympathetic, or general, strike. This asked for all workers to show their support of the metalworkers and building tradesmen by walking off the job. On May 15, 1919, 35,000 workers from fifty different unions left their jobs. Streetcars stopped running, and postal workers and telegraphers walked away from their posts. Stores closed down. Essential services including light and water were not interrupted, but Winnipeg was at a standstill. Similar strikes spread across Canada. Strike leaders would not be bullied into going back to work, even with Prime Minister Borden's promise to fire government employees who did not return to work. On June 21, a peaceful march of strikers turned violent. Two men were shot dead by police, thirty-four others were injured, and many leaders and protesters were arrested. By the end of June, the strike was over, six weeks after it began.

1917

Income tax is introduced as a temporary measure, to support the war effort.

1919

The Canadian National Railway is formed.

1920

Japanese Canadians form the Japanese Labour Union.

Economy
1900s

Fox Farming

business was, Dalton secretly mailed the pelts from a distant post office or sent them out at night by ship. Secrets, however, are hard to keep. It was not long before other people became interested. The fox boom had begun. By 1901, there were approximately three hundred fox ranches on the island and the industry was valued at $20 million.

The Growth of Wheat

"King Wheat" provided approximately 40 percent of Canada's exports. Improved grains that matured earlier, better farming techniques and machinery, and higher prices for wheat helped make western farmers prosperous. Farmers increased the amount of land under cultivation over the decade from 15.4 million to 57.7 million acres. Wheat was so important that many people predicted that in less than 50 years, Saskatchewan and Alberta would both have more people than Ontario.

Fox Farming

The stink from the fox farms was a welcome smell. Although Prince Edward Island's economy, like the rest of the Maritimes, was in a poor state, fox farming prospered. At the end of the nineteenth century, black foxes were very rare and their pelts were valuable. The guard hairs of the black fox are tipped with silver, giving rise to the term "silver fox." Robert Oulton and Charles Dalton realized they could make a fortune if they could somehow breed black foxes the same way farmers bred cows and horses. To make fox kennels, they nailed a board over one end of a hollow log and filled the log with soft, dry seaweed. To prevent the captive foxes from using their sharp teeth and claws to escape into the woods, the men built fences. Part of each fence was buried deep in the soil so the foxes could not escape by digging under the fence.

Male and female foxes were kept separate except at breeding time. And since a mother fox might kill her young if she was disturbed during **whelping** season, quiet was essential. Finally, they were successful. A single pelt sold for $1,800 in London, England. The partners wanted to keep their success a secret. They did not even tell their wives and children about the details of the breeding. They discouraged visitors to the ranch and hired a guard to protect the grounds at night. So that no one would discover how valuable the

The Growth of Wheat

Children's Work

Every small prairie town along the railway lines had a colourful wooden grain elevator. These structures, which towered 30 metres into the sky, were distinctive symbols of prairie architecture. The farmers stored their grain in these elevators, where it was weighed, cleaned, and later loaded onto railway boxcars for export to world markets.

1900

Children's Work

Farm work was difficult. Farmers butchered their own meat and churned their own butter. Children provided much needed manual labour. Their work was often essential for the economic survival of the family. Edith Williams from Nova Scotia describes part of her summer holidays in 1900. "When the little one-roomed schoolhouse was closed for the summer holiday, all boys and girls had special work planned. Everyone worked for a living, children included....The fishermen had to salt their fish, then dry them for market late in the fall. Everything seemed to be the hard way, but taken for granted as part of their living. So there was fish to be washed, pressed, dried and tended on the flakes or rocks. Hay had to be made for winter feed for the cattle. I worked with Owen, [her brother] who said we made a 'good team.' ...A fine sunny day meant working in the hayfield or weeding the garden. I remember weeding the vegetable garden until dusk, after which my lunch was a thick slice of bread and molasses with a glass of fresh buttermilk while I rested weary bones on the big rock by our back door."

1900

Regional Wealth

Canada's economy relied on natural products. With a population of 5.3 million people in 1900, Canada had grown a great deal since Confederation. As immigrants continued to pour into western Canada, farmers produced huge quantities of grains, butter, and other dairy products. The factories in central Canada worked full-time, producing agricultural machines, pulp and paper, boots and shoes, and clothing. The earth provided copper, iron, coal and nickel. Although Nova Scotia produced half of Canada's steel, the economy of the Maritimes did not keep pace with the rest of the country. Thousands of Maritimers left their homes for jobs in the United States or western Canada. In the Alberta foothills, cattle ranching was dominant. Salmon fishing was profitable on the west coast. The Klondike produced gold. Prospectors discovered silver in northern Ontario. Coal was mined in Nova Scotia, Alberta, and British Columbia. Wheat was king on the prairies. The end of the 19th century was a time of extremes. There was crippling poverty and lavish wealth. The wealthiest businessmen lived in huge, mansions, complete with stained glass windows, large ballrooms, elevators, fountains, and coaches with footmen. William Van Horne of the Canadian Pacific Railway bought paintings worth $3 million. Others had their own private railway cars, and Henry Pellatt, hydropower **magnate**, built his own castle, called Castle Loma, in Toronto.

Regional Wealth

1906
Ontario Hydro begins operations.

1907
Stellarton, Nova Scotia becomes home to the first Sobeys grocery store.

1908
The Royal Canadian Mint is established.

45

ACTIVITY
Into the future

The economy is affected by many factors that create constant changes. For a government to run effectively, it must impose taxes on the people who live in the country. Taxes are used in a variety of ways, such as paying the salaries of elected representatives or funding road repairs. To cover the cost of these items, the government taxes income, purchases, and properties. Imagine that you are an economist, and you have been hired to help the government find a fair way to tax certain items. Based on what you have learned in this book, think about how you would tax items based on where they were made, as well as other factors. Do they pay income or property tax?

Become an Economist

Over the next week, make a list of items that are taxed and at what percentage. Most receipts will include the amount of tax paid on a separate line. How much tax do you pay on food? What percent of sales tax is charged on clothing? When your parents fill up their car with fuel, how much tax do they pay? Talk to an adult, such as a parent or teacher, about the ways they pay taxes. Be sure to use the amount before taxes for your calculation. Next, use a calculator to determine how much tax you would pay on a certain item. For example, if you paid $1.21 in taxes on a restaurant bill for $20.17, divide 20.17 by 1.21 to calculate the tax. On this bill, you paid 0.0599, which rounds to 0.06. Percent means "one per hundred," so 0.06 is equal to 6 percent. Once you have made a list of items, compare the percent of tax paid on each. Are all of the items taxed the same? If not, why do you think they are taxed differently? Is this fair?

FURTHER
Research

Many books and websites provide information on the Canadian economy. To learn more about this topic, borrow books from the library, or surf the Internet.

Books

Most libraries have computers that connect to a database for researching information. If you input a key word, you will be provided with a list of books in the library that contain information on that topic. Non-fiction books are arranged numerically, using their call number. Fiction books are organized alphabetically by the author's last name.

Websites

To learn more about the Canadian economy, visit **http://canadianeconomy.gc.ca/english/economy/index.cfm**.

For additional information about the Canadian economy, surf to **www.economywatch.com/world_economy/canada**.

| Français | Contact Us | Help | Search | Canada Site |
| | | Home | Site Map | A to Z Index |

Welcome to the
Canadian Economy Online

This one-stop guide to the national economy lets you check out statistics, access a wealth of federal government information and learn more about economic concepts and events.

RESOURCES
Current Economy
Families & Workers
Money
Gov't & the Economy
International Issues
About Business

LEARN ABOUT
Key Indicators
Economic Concepts
Key Economic Events
Economy Overview
Other Useful Links

RETURN
Home

CHECK THIS OUT
Weekly Statistics
Budget 2007
GST/HST Cuts
Speech from the Throne
Where Your Tax Dollars Go

Pulse of the Economy

Population 2nd quarter 2008	33,223,840
Unemployment rate June 2008	6.2 %
Inflation rate May 2008	2.2 %
Real GDP April 2008, % change	0.4 %
Exports 1st quarter 2008, % change	-1.1 %
Imports 1st quarter 2008, % change	-2.6 %
Exchange rate June 2008 - $CAN buys US$	0.9835
Prime interest rate June 2008	4.75 %
S&P/TSX Composite Index June 2008 (1975=1000)	14,467.03
Federal debt 2007 - $ millions	467,268.0
Retail sales April 2008 , % change	0.6 %
Housing starts June 2008, thousands	217.8
Composite leading indicator June 2008, % change	0.0 %

Last modified: 2008-07-18
Source: Statistics Canada

Check this Out!

Budget 2008

Provincial/Territorial Economic Indicators

New!

Tools

Currency Converter

Inflation Calculator

Glossary

bankruptcy: not being able to repay one's debts

collective bargaining: negotiating for change by an organized group of employees

Confederation: point at which Ontario, Quebec, Nova Scotia, and New Brunswick joined to form Canada

deficit: when a government spends more money than it makes

depression: when the economy of a country is not doing well; unemployment is usually quite high

domestic: within the country

embargo: an official ban on trade with another country

inflation: a sudden drop in the value of money and a rise in prices

magnate: a powerful person in business

revenue: money made from property, investment, and taxes

Tory: another word referring to the Progressive Conservative political party or a member of that party

uranium: a radioactive substance, sometimes used for bombs

whelping: having puppies

Index